THE GREAT SONGS OF GERSHWIN ®

GERSHWIN® and **GEORGE GERSHWIN®**
are registered trademarks of Gershwin Enterprises
All Rights Reserved

CONTENTS

BIDIN' MY TIME

Music and Lyrics by
GEORGE GERSHWIN
and IRA GERSHWIN

Some fel-lers love to "Tip-Toe Through the Tu-lips;"_____

Some fel-lers go on "Sing - ing In The Rain."_____

Some fel-lers keep on "Paint-in' Skies With Sun-Shine."_____

5

HOW LONG HAS THIS BEEN GOING ON?

Music and Lyrics by
GEORGE GERSHWIN
and IRA GERSHWIN

He: As a tot, when I trot-ted in lit-tle vel-vet pant-ies,
She: 'Neath the stars at ba-zaars of-ten I've had to ca-ress men,

I was kissed by my sis-ters, my cous-ins and my aunt-ies.
Five or ten dol-lars then I'd col-lect from all those yes-men.

Sad to tell, it was Hell, an in-fer-no worse than Dan-te's.
Don't be sad, I must add that they meant no more than chess-men.

LOOKING FOR A BOY

Music and Lyrics by
GEORGE GERSHWIN
and IRA GERSHWIN

MINE

Music and Lyrics by
GEORGE GERSHWIN
and IRA GERSHWIN

Wor-ried to-geth-er, Strug-gled to-geth-er, Stood to-geth-er, to-geth-er,

I grow so sen-ti-men-tal, I'm a-fraid I've got to burst in-to

song. *All:* Please do. We'd love to know how you

feel a-bout her, And how she feels a-bout you.

Slowly, with much expression
1st Refrain:

18

19

BY STRAUSS

Music and Lyrics by
GEORGE GERSHWIN
and IRA GERSHWIN

Oh, I'd give no quar-ter to Kern or Cole Por-ter and

Gersh-win keeps pound-ing on tin._____ How can I be

civ-il when hear - ing this driv - el? It's on - ly for

night club-bing sous - es._____ Oh, give me the free 'n' eas - y

FUNNY FACE

Music and Lyrics by
GEORGE GERSHWIN
and IRA GERSHWIN

27

THE MAN I LOVE

Music and Lyrics by
GEORGE GERSHWIN
and IRA GERSHWIN

SWEET AND LOW-DOWN

Music and Lyrics by
GEORGE GERHWIN
and IRA GERSHWIN

There's a cab-a-ret in this cit-y___ I can rec-om-mend to you; Peps you up like e-lec-tric-i-ty___ When the band is blow-ing "blue." They play noth-ing clas-sic, oh no! down there;

36

NICE WORK IF YOU CAN GET IT

Music and Lyrics by
GEORGE GERSHWIN
and IRA GERSHWIN

The man who on-ly lives for mak-ing mon-ey Lives a life that is-n't nec-es-sa-ri-ly sun-ny. Like-wise the man who works for fame,

Nice Work If You Can Get It, And you can get it if you try.

Just im-ag-ine some - one Wait - ing at the cot - tage door,

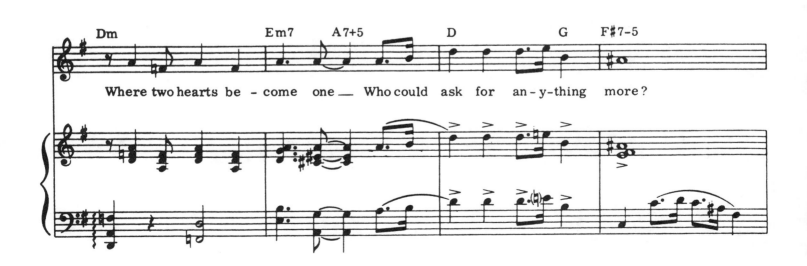

Where two hearts be - come one Who could ask for an - y-thing more?

42

THAT CERTAIN FEELING

Music and Lyrics by
GEORGE GERSHWIN
and IRA GERSHWIN

REFRAIN

DELISHIOUS

Music and Lyrics by
GEORGE GERSHWIN
and IRA GERSHWIN

What can I say___ To sing my praise of you?___ I must re-veal___ The things I feel.___ What can I say?___ Each love-ly

48

LOVE IS HERE TO STAY

Music and Lyrics by
GEORGE GERSHWIN
and IRA GERSHWIN

The more I read the pa-pers The less I com-pre-hend The

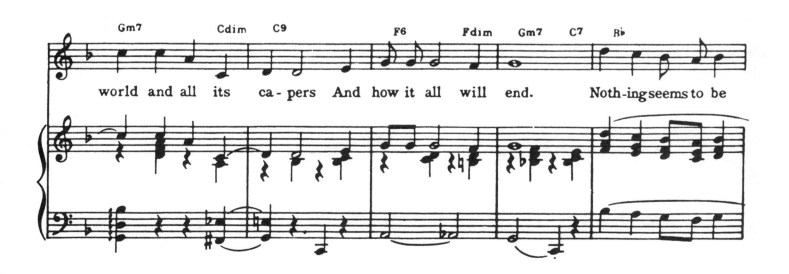

world and all its ca-pers And how it all will end. Noth-ing seems to be

52

A FOGGY DAY

Music and Lyrics by
GEORGE GERSHWIN
and IRA GERSHWIN

Moderato

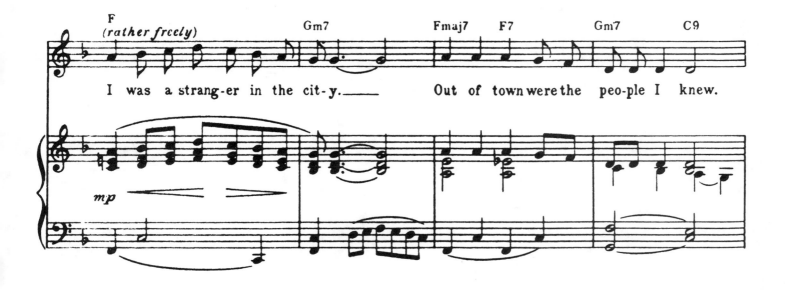

I was a strang-er in the cit-y.____ Out of town were the peo-ple I knew.

I had that feel-ing of self - pi-ty, ____ What to do? What to do? What to do? The

55

56

THE BABBIT AND THE BROMIDE

From "Funny Face"

Music and Lyrics by
GEORGE GERSHWIN
and IRA GERSHWIN

59

SWANEE

Words by
IRVING CAESAR

Music by
GEORGE GERSHWIN

64

65

CLAP YO' HANDS

Music and Lyrics by
GEORGE GERSHWIN
and IRA GERSHWIN

IT AIN'T NECESSARILY SO

By
GEORGE GERSHWIN,
DU BOSE and DOROTHY HEYWARD
and IRA GERSHWIN

72

LOVE WALKED IN

Music and Lyrics by
GEORGE GERSHWIN
and IRA GERSHWIN

Moderato

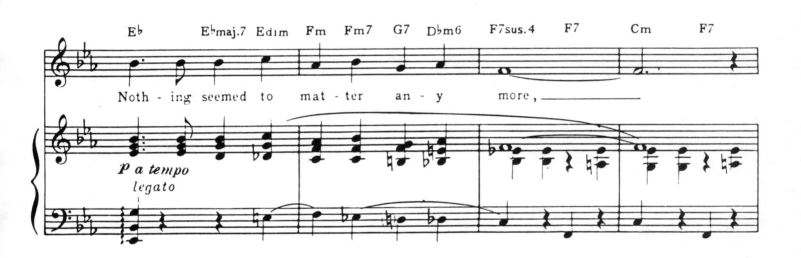

Noth - ing seemed to mat - ter an - y more, ____

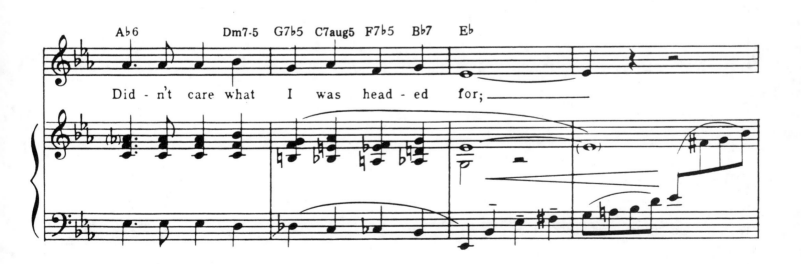

Did - n't care what I was head - ed for; ____

Time was stand-ing still, Noth-ing count-ed till There

came a knock-knock-knock-ing at the door. ____

Refrain *(slowly, with much expression)*

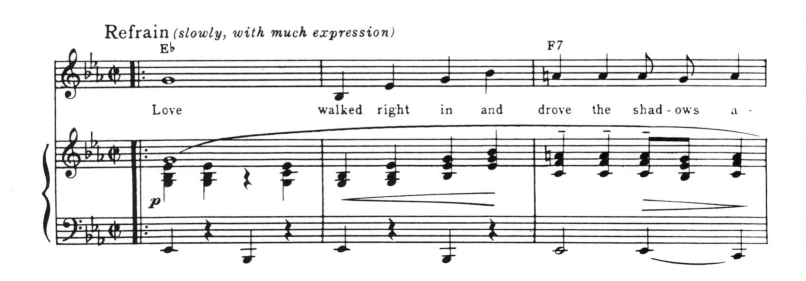

Love walked right in and drove the shad-ows a-

78

WHO CARES?
(SO LONG AS YOU CARE FOR ME)

Music and Lyrics by
GEORGE GERSHWIN
and IRA GERSHWIN

Let it rain and thun-der! Let a mil-lion

firms go un-der! I am not con-cerned with

Refrain

(in a lilting manner)

DO, DO, DO

Music and Lyrics by
GEORGE GERSHWIN
and IRA GERSHWIN

86

LET'S CALL THE WHOLE THING OFF

Music and Lyrics by
GEORGE GERSHWIN
and IRA GERSHWIN

Allegretto

Brightly

Things have come to a pret-ty pass,— Our ro-mance is grow-ing flat, For you like this and the oth-er— While

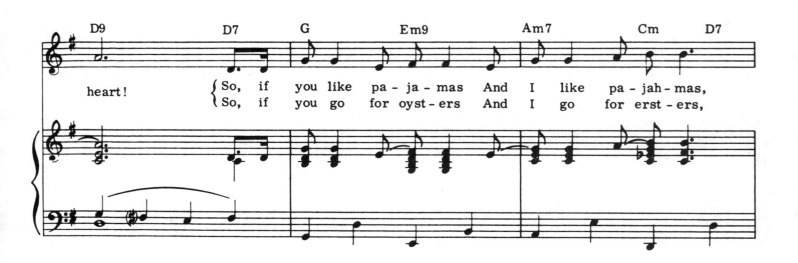

'S WONDERFUL

Music and Lyrics by
GEORGE GERSHWIN
and IRA GERSHWIN

Moderato

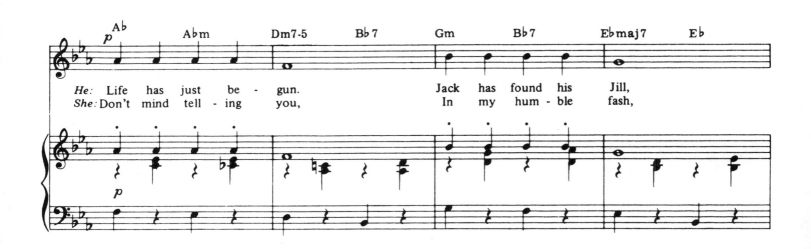

He: Life has just be - gun. Jack has found his Jill,
She: Don't mind tell - ing you, In my hum - ble fash,

Don't know what you've done, But I'm all a - thrill.
That you thrill me through With a ten - der pash.

STRIKE UP THE BAND

Music and Lyrics by
GEORGE GERSHWIN
and IRA GERSHWIN

100

FASCINATING RHYTHM

Music and Lyrics by
GEORGE GERSHWIN
and IRA GERSHWIN

Got a lit-tle rhy-thm, A rhy-thm, a rhy-thm That pit-a-pats through my brain. So darn per-sis-tent, The day is-n't dis-tant When it-'ll drive me in - sane. Comes in the morn-ing With-

I'VE GOT A CRUSH ON YOU

Music and Lyrics by
GEORGE GERSHWIN
and IRA GERSHWIN

wore down my re-sist-ance: I fell, _____ and it was swell. _____

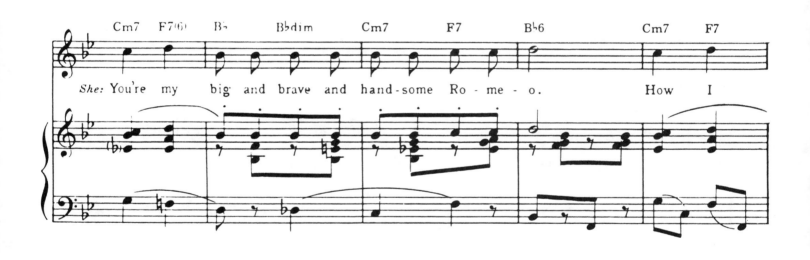

She: You're my big and brave and hand-some Ro-me-o. How I

won you I shall nev-er, nev-er know. *He:* It's not that you're at-trac-tive, But

MAYBE

Music and Lyrics by
GEORGE GERSHWIN
and IRA GERSHWIN

Though to-day is a blue day Still to-mor-row is near, And per-haps with the new day

111

BUT NOT FOR ME

Music and Lyrics by
GEORGE GERSHWIN
and IRA GERSHWIN

Moderato

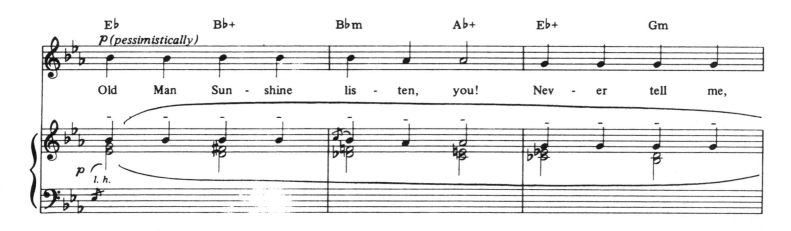

Old Man Sun - shine lis - ten, you! Nev - er tell me,

"Dreams come true!" Just try it And I'll start a ri - ot.

116

117

SOMEBODY LOVES ME

Words by
BALLARD MACDONALD and B.G. DeSYLVA
French version by EMELIA RENAUD

Music by
GEORGE GERSHWIN

Allegro moderato

When this world be - gan   It was Heav - en's   plan,
Tout dès le dé - but   Il fut en - ten - du

There should be a   girl for ev - 'ry   sin - gle   man;
Qu'il y au - rait   pour chaque hom-me   u - ne   femme;

To my great re - gret   Some - one has up - set, ___
Mais à mon re - gret   Fut chan - gé l'as - pect

121

AREN'T YOU KIND OF GLAD WE DID?

Music and Lyrics by
GEORGE GERSHWIN
and IRA GERSHWIN

I'LL BUILD A STAIRWAY TO PARADISE

Words by
B.G. DeSYLVA and IRA GERSHWIN

Music by
GEORGE GERSHWIN

128

129

LOVE IS SWEEPING THE COUNTRY

Music and Lyrics by
GEORGE GERSHWIN
and IRA GERSHWIN

Why are peo-ple gay All the night and day, Feel-ing as they nev-er felt be-fore? What is the thing That makes them sing?

132

SOMEONE TO WATCH OVER ME

Music and Lyrics by
GEORGE GERSHWIN
and IRA GERSHWIN

Lyrics:
There's a say-ing old Says that love is blind, Still we're of-ten told, "Seek and ye shall find." So I'm going to seek A cer-tain lad I've had in mind.

135

136

MY ONE AND ONLY (What Am I Gonna Do)

Music and Lyrics by
GEORGE GERSHWIN
and IRA GERSHWIN

139

YOU'VE GOT WHAT GETS ME

Music and Lyrics by
GEORGE GERSHWIN
and IRA GERSHWIN

I've got a se - cret that I can con - ceal no long - er,___

___ And you're the one that I sim - ply must tell it

BESS, YOU IS MY WOMAN NOW

By
GEORGE GERSHWIN,
DU BOSE and DOROTHY HEYWARD
and IRA GERSHWIN

147

149

151

154

FOR YOU, FOR ME, FOREVERMORE

Music and Lyrics by
GEORGE GERSHWIN
and IRA GERSHWIN

LIZA (All The Clouds'll Roll Away)

Words by
GUS KAHN and IRA GERSHWIN

Music by
GEORGE GERSHWIN

160

But if you'll smile on me   All the clouds -'ll roll a -

way.   Li - za,   Li - za,   don't de -

lay,   Come, keep me com - pa - ny,   And the clouds -'ll roll a -

way.   See   the hon - ey - moon a - shin - in'

EMBRACEABLE YOU

Music and Lyrics by
GEORGE GERSHWIN
and IRA GERSHWIN

164

BLAH-BLAH-BLAH

Music and Lyrics by
GEORGE GERSHWIN
and IRA GERSHWIN

learned it from the screen. (I hope you like it.) _____ I

stud - ied all the rhymes that all the lov - ers sing; _____ then

just for you I wrote this lit - tle thing. _____

Refrain:

Blah, blah, blah, blah moon, blah, blah, blah a - bove,

SOON

Music and Lyrics by
GEORGE GERSHWIN
and IRA GERSHWIN

He: I'm mak-ing up for all the years that I wait-ed, I'm com-pen-sat-ed at last.

My heart is through with shirk-ing, dear, through you it's work-ing

OF THEE I SING
(BABY)

Music and Lyrics by
GEORGE GERSHWIN
and IRA GERSHWIN

Assai moderato

From the Is-land of Man-hat-tan to the Coast of Gold, From North to South, From East to West, You are the love I love the best.

177

THEY CAN'T TAKE THAT AWAY FROM ME

Music and Lyrics by
GEORGE GERSHWIN
and IRA GERSHWIN

ISN'T IT A PITY

From "Pardon My English"

Music and Lyrics by
GEORGE GERSHWIN
and IRA GERSHWIN

OH, LADY BE GOOD!

Music and Lyrics by
GEORGE GERSHWIN
and IRA GERSHWIN

HIGH HAT

Music and Lyrics by
GEORGE GERSHWIN
and IRA GERSHWIN

Allegro moderato

He: When a fel - low feels he's got to win a girl - ie's hand - ie,

he will send her loads of flow - ers, books and tons of can - dy. *Chorus:* The

o - ver - head is big; oh, how they make us dig!

I GOT PLENTY O' NUTTIN'

By
GEORGE GERSHWIN,
DU BOSE and DOROTHY HEYWARD
and IRA GERSHWIN

195

DO IT AGAIN !

Words by
B.G. DeSYLVA

Music by
GEORGE GERSHWIN

LET'S KISS AND MAKE UP

Music and Lyrics by
GEORGE GERSHWIN
and IRA GERSHWIN

FIDGETY FEET

Music and Lyrics by
GEORGE GERSHWIN
and IRA GERSHWIN

I GOT RHYTHM

Music and Lyrics by
GEORGE GERSHWIN
and IRA GERSHWIN

214

REFRAIN (*with abandon*)

HE LOVES AND SHE LOVES

Music and Lyrics by
GEORGE GERSHWIN
and IRA GERSHWIN

THEY ALL LAUGHED

Music and Lyrics by
GEORGE GERSHWIN
and IRA GERSHWIN

224